HIP-HOP STYLE

FASHION FORWARD

Dr. Monica B. Morall-Baker
Cicely Lewis, Executive Editor

LERNER PUBLICATIONS ◆ MINNEAPOLIS

LETTER FROM CICELY LEWIS

Dear Reader,

Hip-hop has been a part of my life from an early age. I remember using my brush as a microphone and rapping along with Salt-N-Pepa. Hip-hop influenced my fashion, way of speaking, and lifestyle. As a teacher, I shared Tupac's writings to teach poetry elements and Queen Latifah's "U.N.I.T.Y." to help my students better understand the works of poet Maya Angelou.

CICELY LEWIS

As a librarian, I want to expose my students to literature that empowers them to take action and that amplifies voices of underrepresented groups. That is what hip-hop does. Hip-hop is more than beats and rhymes; it's a cultural force. For Black people, it's been a spotlight on social justice, and a canvas for our frustrations, joys, and creativity.

As you read the series, think about the power of hip-hop and how it all began. You've probably heard of Cardi B and Nicki Minaj, but who paved the way for them? Reflect on how this musical genre that began in the Black Community is now present around the world.

—Cicely Lewis, Executive Editor

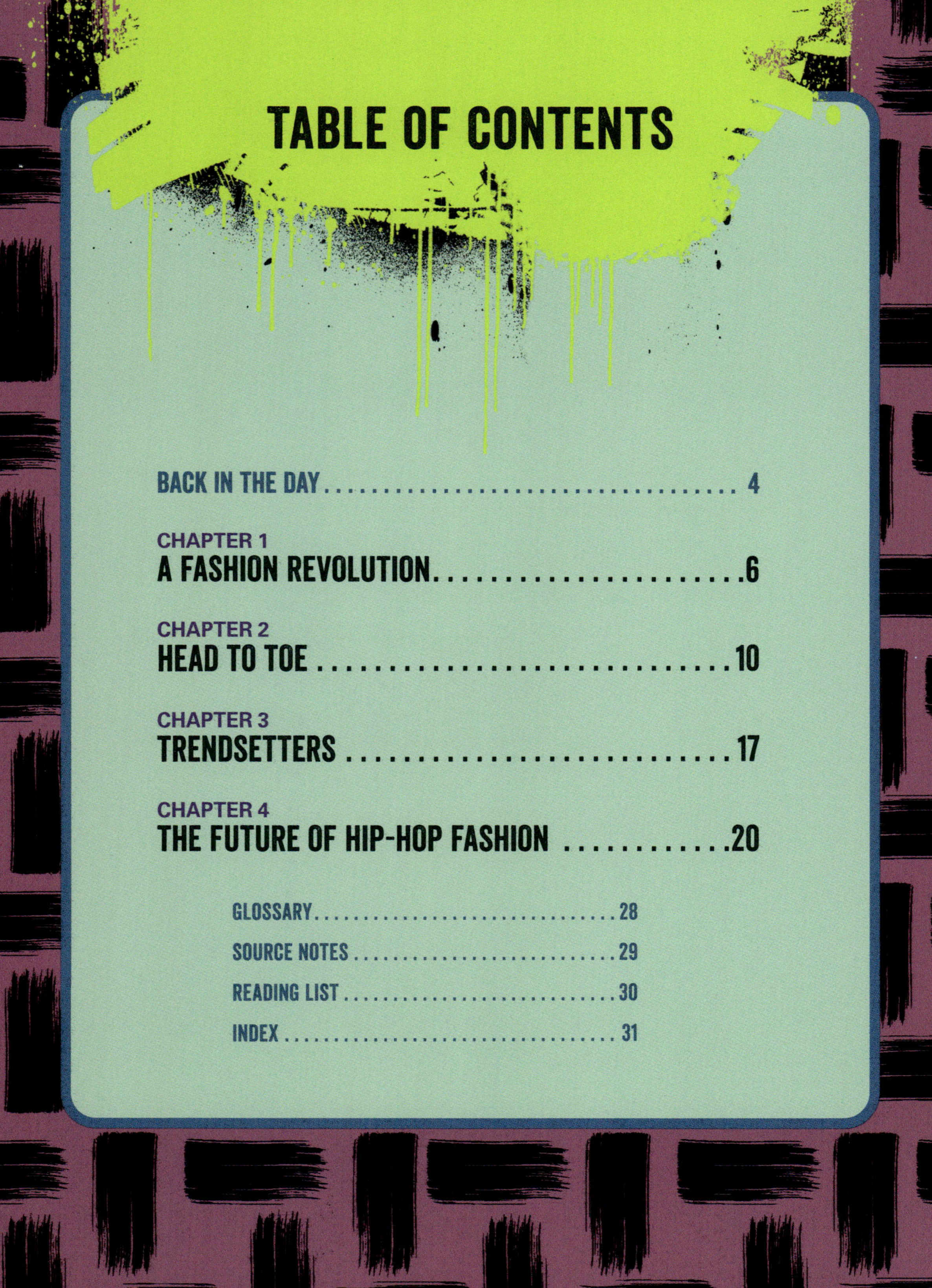

TABLE OF CONTENTS

BACK IN THE DAY

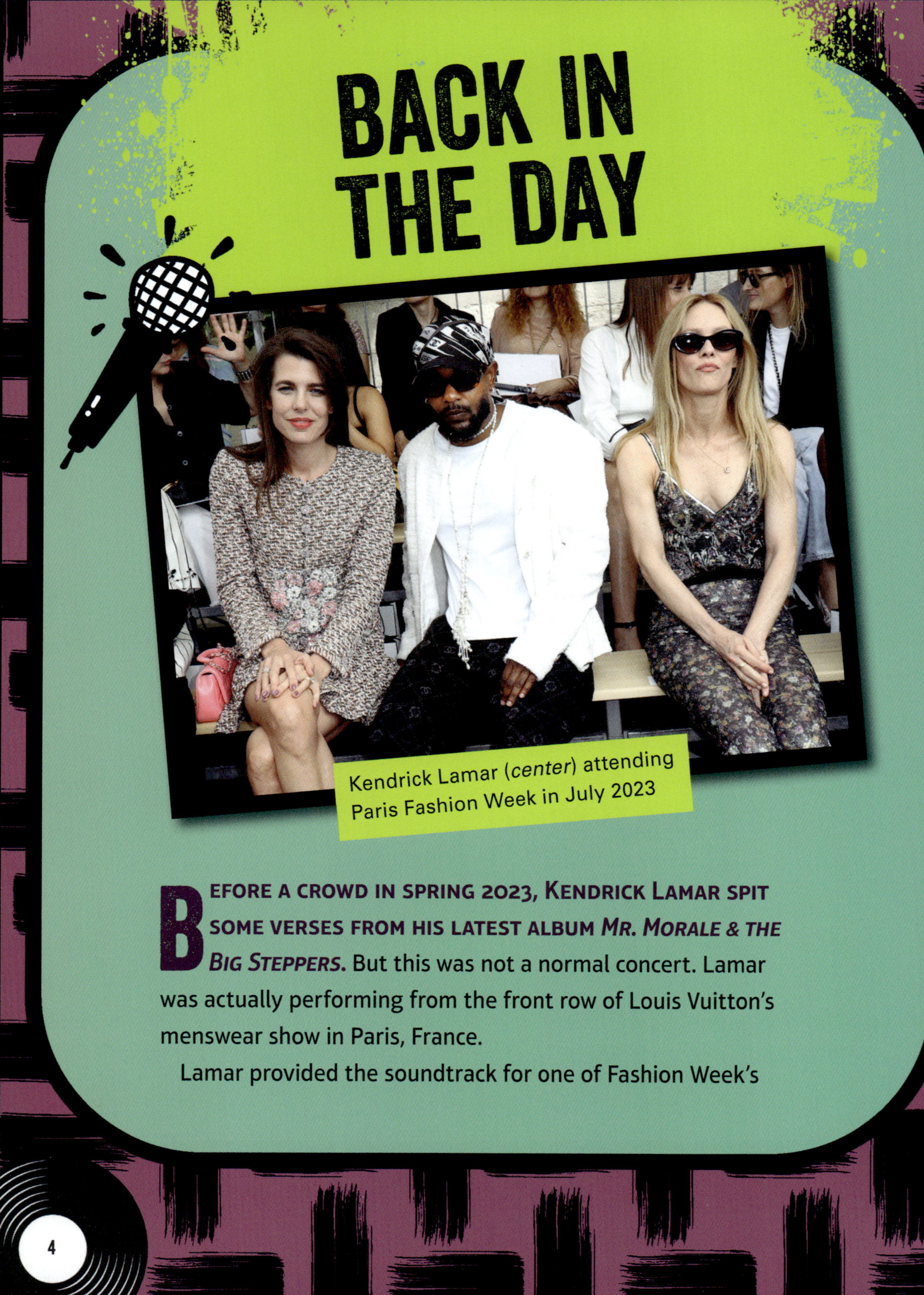

Kendrick Lamar (*center*) attending Paris Fashion Week in July 2023

BEFORE A CROWD IN SPRING 2023, KENDRICK LAMAR SPIT SOME VERSES FROM HIS LATEST ALBUM *MR. MORALE & THE BIG STEPPERS.* But this was not a normal concert. Lamar was actually performing from the front row of Louis Vuitton's menswear show in Paris, France.

Lamar provided the soundtrack for one of Fashion Week's

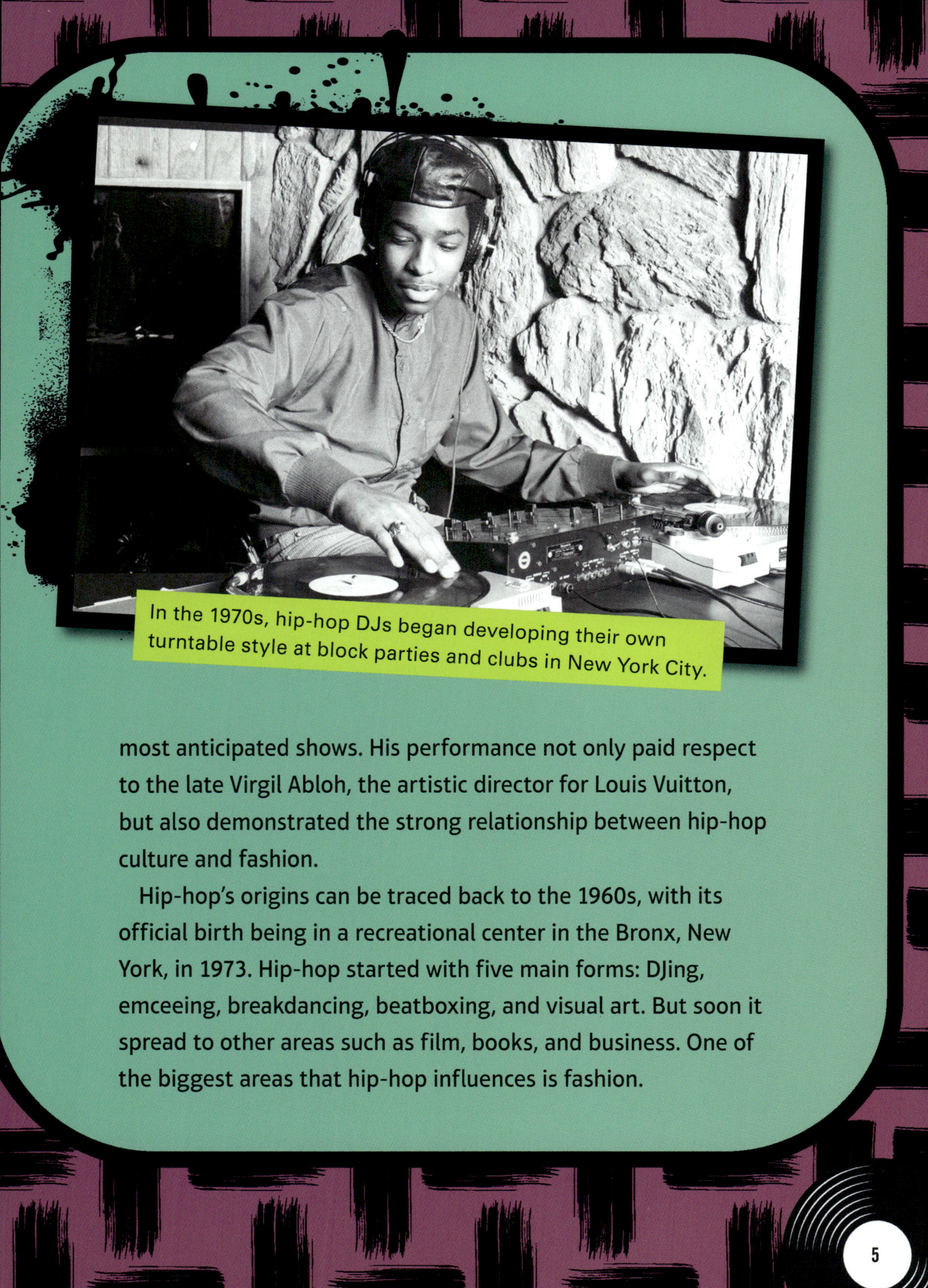

In the 1970s, hip-hop DJs began developing their own turntable style at block parties and clubs in New York City.

most anticipated shows. His performance not only paid respect to the late Virgil Abloh, the artistic director for Louis Vuitton, but also demonstrated the strong relationship between hip-hop culture and fashion.

Hip-hop's origins can be traced back to the 1960s, with its official birth being in a recreational center in the Bronx, New York, in 1973. Hip-hop started with five main forms: DJing, emceeing, breakdancing, beatboxing, and visual art. But soon it spread to other areas such as film, books, and business. One of the biggest areas that hip-hop influences is fashion.

CHAPTER 1

A FASHION REVOLUTION

A group of breakdancers in 1984

HIP-HOP FASHION BEGAN AS A FORM OF SELF-EXPRESSION FOR YOUNG PEOPLE. Dance, art, and more have influenced the way hip-hop fashion is presented and evolving.

Breakdancing was created by Black and Latin communities in the Bronx, New York, in the 1970s.

BREAKING OUT

Breakdancing, or breaking, is an energetic style of street dance that includes acrobatic or athletic moves. It is often performed to hip-hop music. People who breakdance are called b-boys, b-girls, or breakers.

Breakdancing was one of the early influences of hip-hop fashion. To move more easily, dancers wore baggy clothing, such as oversized pants, jackets, hoodies, and tracksuits. This comfortable style soon became a big part of hip-hop fashion.

ARTIST'S SPARK

Graffiti is writing or art drawn without permission in a public space, such as on a wall or railway. Hip-hop's connection to

Breakdancers performing in front of a wall of graffiti

graffiti can be traced to the 1960s in New York City, where hip-hop music was growing at the time.

People often graffiti as a response to a social, political, or cultural issue. Graffiti artists spray bright colors and bold patterns on buildings and subway trains. Soon these same designs were on the clothing of young hip-hop fans.

REFLECT

Breakdancing and graffiti art were both major cultural influences on early hip-hop fashion. What cultural influences do you see on hip-hop fashion?

FASHIONING A CONNECTION

Emcees rap or create rhymes over hip-hop music. Sometimes, the emcees gave shoutouts to the clothing brands that they were wearing. For example, Ricky Walters, a.k.a. Slick Rick, shouted out Bally shoes and Kangol hats in his 1985 song "La-Di-Da-Di." Fans of the emcee would then buy these brands. Fashion became a way for fans to connect with their favorite artists.

Slick Rick (*left*) performs onstage with beatboxer Doug E. Fresh (*right*) in 1985.

CHAPTER 2

HEAD TO TOE

Rap icon LL Cool J attends the Video Music Awards in August 2022.

ACCESSORIES ARE AN IMPORTANT PART OF HIP-HOP FASHION. From hats to jewelry to sneakers, having the freshest accessories to complete one's fit is key to looking the part.

HIP HATS

The Kangol hat is a round hat with a short brim. This hat became popular in hip-hop when rap pioneers Kurtis Blow and LL Cool J wore it on their album covers in the late 1980s. In 2002 rapper Missy Elliot wore a fuzzy version of the Kangol hat for the cover of her album.

Missy Elliot wearing a fuzzy, pink Kangol hat at the 2005 Olympus Fashion Week

THE KANGAROO HAT

The Kangol hat was first worn by British soldiers during World War II (1939–1945). In 1983 the Kangol company added the famous kangaroo logo because people kept asking for the "kangaroo hat."

General Bernard Montgomery of the British Army wearing a beret created by Kangol in 1943

Big Daddy Kane wearing trunk jewelry in 1988

GOT THAT BLING

The word *bling* became popular after rapper Lil Wayne used it in a song to describe flashy jewelry worn by hip-hop artists. But before that, rappers in the mid-1980s such as LL Cool J and Big Daddy Kane wore trunk jewelry. Trunk jewelry is mostly heavy, gold or gold-plated jewelry. It includes custom-made pieces such as multi-fingered rings and large nameplates hanging from thick gold chains. These represent wealth, status, and success.

A RAPPER'S REGRET

Many people credit New Orleans rapper Lil Wayne with coining the term *bling*. It was made popular by his song from 1999. He has often expressed regret for not trademarking the word.

Lil Wayne at a music festival in 2019

Early female emcees such as Roxanne Shante and Salt-N-Pepa wore large gold earrings. They were called bamboo earrings or door knockers. Some people say that the heavy gold jewelry imitates jewelry that was worn by people in ancient Africa.

> **"This goes back to Africa. The gold chains are basically for warriors. Right now, the artists in the rap field are battling. We're the head warriors."**
>
> **—Schoolly D, 1988**

SNEAKER STYLE

One of the most popular hip-hop accessories are sneakers. Hip-hop trio Run-DMC often wore shell-toe Adidas sneakers with no laces. Run-DMC made the sportswear brand even more popular by writing the song "My Adidas."

In the 1980s, Nike reached out to superstar athlete Michael Jordan. He would become the face of a new shoe line, Air Jordan. Their collaboration changed the hip-hop shoe game forever. Artists and fans alike wore the new Air Jordan. Rapper Nelly added to the Nike frenzy with his 2002 hit "Air Force Ones."

TAILORED TOES

Sneakers were not the only shoes made popular by hip-hop. By the 1990s, Timberland boots, also known as Timbs, became popular among hip-hop stars. Artists such as The Notorious B.I.G., Mobb Deep, and the Wu-Tang Clan wore them at performances and on album covers.

Raekwon of the Wu-Tang Clan posing with his Timberland boots

At first, Timberland did not want to be connected to hip-hop, but they soon changed their minds. Their sales greatly increased between the early 1990s and the early 2000s. Leaders at Timberland said that its success was mostly because of the support of Black communities.

REFLECT

At first, Timberland executives did not want to be associated with the hip-hop community. Why do you think they felt this way? What are some things that could have influenced them to change their minds?

CHAPTER 3

TRENDSETTERS

Queen Latifah sings onstage in Las Vegas, Nevada, in 2003.

NO ONE PERSON CREATED HIP-HOP FASHION, BUT MANY ARTISTS HAVE INFLUENCED ITS TRENDS OVER THE YEARS. From LL Cool J to Queen Latifah, hip-hop trendsetters have always made a mark in the fashion world.

INSPIRING ICONS

In the early years of hip-hop, artists copied styles from disco music. Groups such as Grandmaster Flash and the Furious Five often wore flashy costumes with leather and tall boots.

Then, in the 1980s, Run-DMC and LL Cool J helped make streetwear fashion popular. Run-DMC traded their corduroy suits and plaid sports jackets for Adidas tracksuits. The trio paired the tracksuits with matching sneakers that had no laces.

In the 1980s, rap artists began wearing fashion that represented African culture. Kool Moe Dee and Queen Latifah wore kufis. These round, brimless caps often have patterns or symbols that demonstrate cultural pride. Artists also wore African-inspired patterns, pendants, and jewelry.

Run-DMC was one of the most iconic hip-hop groups in the 1980s.

COURTSIDE CRAZE

Sports had a big influence on hip-hop fashion. In the late 1990s and early 2000s, artists such as Outkast and Nelly wore throwback jerseys at performances and on album covers. These jerseys are like the jerseys pro sports players wore in the past for basketball or football. After being worn by big artists, the throwback jersey exploded in popularity.

Baseball caps are also a popular hip-hop accessory. These became popular in hip-hop fashion in the 1980s. Performers such as Offset from the Migos wear New Era fitted caps to support their favorite teams while rocking the mic onstage.

Nelly wearing a throwback jersey while attending an award show in Pasadena, California, in 2002

CHAPTER 4

THE FUTURE OF HIP-HOP FASHION

Models walk down the runway for FUBU at Atlanta Fashion Week in October 2024.

IN THE EARLY DAYS OF HIP-HOP, ARTISTS' STYLES WERE INSPIRED BY THEIR ENVIRONMENTS AND EXISTING FASHIONS. Since then, street styles that are created for function and ease have become a major part of everyday fashion.

FASHION FLOOD

Around the 1990s, some hip-hop artists and entrepreneurs began creating their own fashion brands. Companies such as FUBU, Karl Kani, and Cross Colours took over the hip-hop fashion industry. They flooded the market with bright colors, bold designs, and oversized shapes. The styles were popular with hip-hop fans everywhere.

PHAT FASHION

In 1992 business owner Russell Simmons created the clothing company Phat Farm. Phat Farm combined a preppy style with hip-hop. Its success led to the company branching out with more brands.

Fashion designer Kimora Lee Simmons became the president and creative designer of Phat Farm's new brand, Baby Phat, in 2000. This label combined

Kimora Lee Simmons at Baby Phat's sneaker launch party in June 2004

women's fashion with hip-hop and streetwear. Artists such as Missy Elliot and Lil' Kim regularly wore clothes and accessories from Baby Phat.

In 2019 Simmons relaunched Baby Phat. Her two daughters, Ming and Aoki, helped her. This rebrand put its new collection in Forever 21 stores. In 2022 Baby Phat began a new partnership with Macy's and Puma athletic wear.

From left to right: Aoki Lee Simmons, Kimora Lee Simmons, and Ming Lee Simmons at New York Fashion Week in 2023

REFLECT

Many celebrities such as Megan Thee Stallion and Cardi B wear clothes from popular fashion companies. How might this positively affect the fashion company?

WEARING WALKER

In 1987 fashion designer April Walker opened her first fashion line out of her home in Brooklyn, New York. Her clothing line Walker Wear took off. She dressed artists such as The Notorious B.I.G., Tupac, Run-DMC, and Aaliyah. This helped her brand become more popular. Walker has since partnered with schools and funded scholarships for people interested in streetwear fashion design.

"I want to leave an imprint on the world where when young Black and Brown people, specifically women, see that I did this in 1987, they absolutely can shake their head, like, 'Oh, I'm doing this and I can do it bigger and better.'"

—April Walker, 2023

Pharrell Williams (*left*) and Nigo wearing glasses the two designed

FASHION FUSION

Hip-hop artist and entrepreneur Pharrell Williams took hip-hop fashion to new levels in 2003. He partnered with Japanese fashion designer Nigo to create the fashion label Billionaire Boys Club. This label combined streetwear with Asian, punk, and skater styles.

REFLECT

Designer April Walker has created several educational partnerships to help future designers and entrepreneurs. Why do you think Walker has dedicated so many resources to this cause?

HIP-HOP TO HIGH-END

In 2016 rapper A$AP Rocky became the first Black American to represent Christian Dior's Dior Homme fashion line, a high-end fashion line. Sometimes, he would call out the names of high-end fashion lines in his songs. This helped strengthen the relationship between hip-hop and high-end fashion.

A$AP Rocky attending Christian Dior's Dior Homme Menswear collection show at Paris Fashion Week in 2018

A FASHION FIRST

Virgil Abloh was the first Black American to hold a top position at Louis Vuitton. He helped transform what high-end hip-hop fashion looked like. He died in 2021, and since then, his foundation awards a "Post-Modern" scholarship each year to support an aspiring designer of Black, African American, or African descent.

Virgil Abloh walks down the runway at the Louis Vuitton showcase at Paris Fashion Week in January 2019.

PASSING IT FORWARD

Fashion thrives best under new innovators. Some organizations have created programs and scholarships to increase the number of Black designers and fashion entrepreneurs. McDonald's USA has partnered with fashion industry leaders to develop educational programs for aspiring Black designers. Hip-hop designer Virgil Abloh began a program that awards scholarships to aspiring Black fashion designers every year.

> **"To me, there's one level of the work that's designing at Louis [Vuitton]. But my real job is to make sure that there's, like, six young Black kids that take my job after me."**
>
> **—Virgil Abloh, 2021**

Now, hip-hop has a front-row seat to the biggest fashion shows in the world. Streetwear inspired by hip-hop culture can be found on the runways of New York; Paris; and Milan, Italy. Hip-hop fashion no longer just influences mainstream culture. It is mainstream culture.

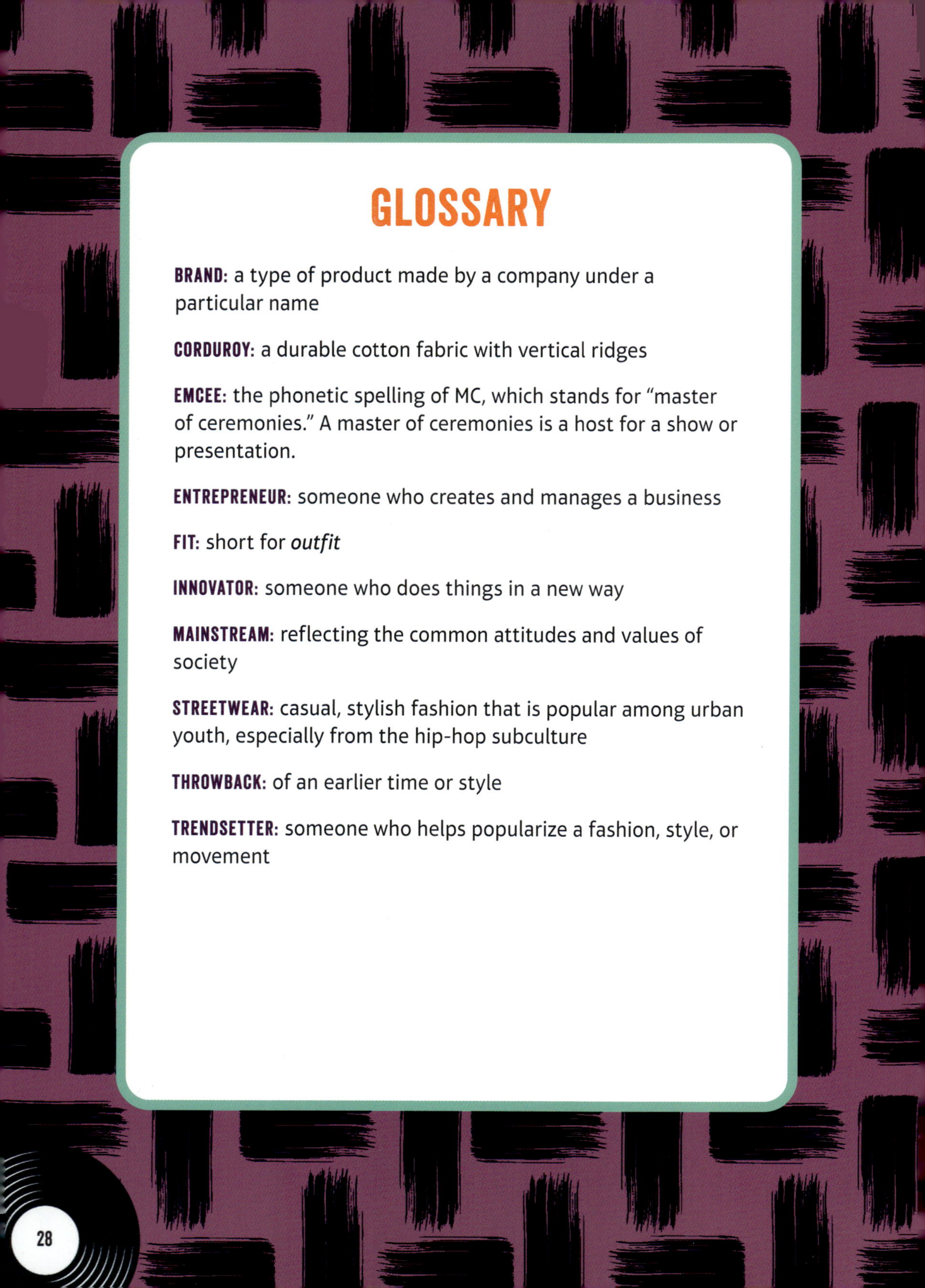

GLOSSARY

BRAND: a type of product made by a company under a particular name

CORDUROY: a durable cotton fabric with vertical ridges

EMCEE: the phonetic spelling of MC, which stands for "master of ceremonies." A master of ceremonies is a host for a show or presentation.

ENTREPRENEUR: someone who creates and manages a business

FIT: short for *outfit*

INNOVATOR: someone who does things in a new way

MAINSTREAM: reflecting the common attitudes and values of society

STREETWEAR: casual, stylish fashion that is popular among urban youth, especially from the hip-hop subculture

THROWBACK: of an earlier time or style

TRENDSETTER: someone who helps popularize a fashion, style, or movement

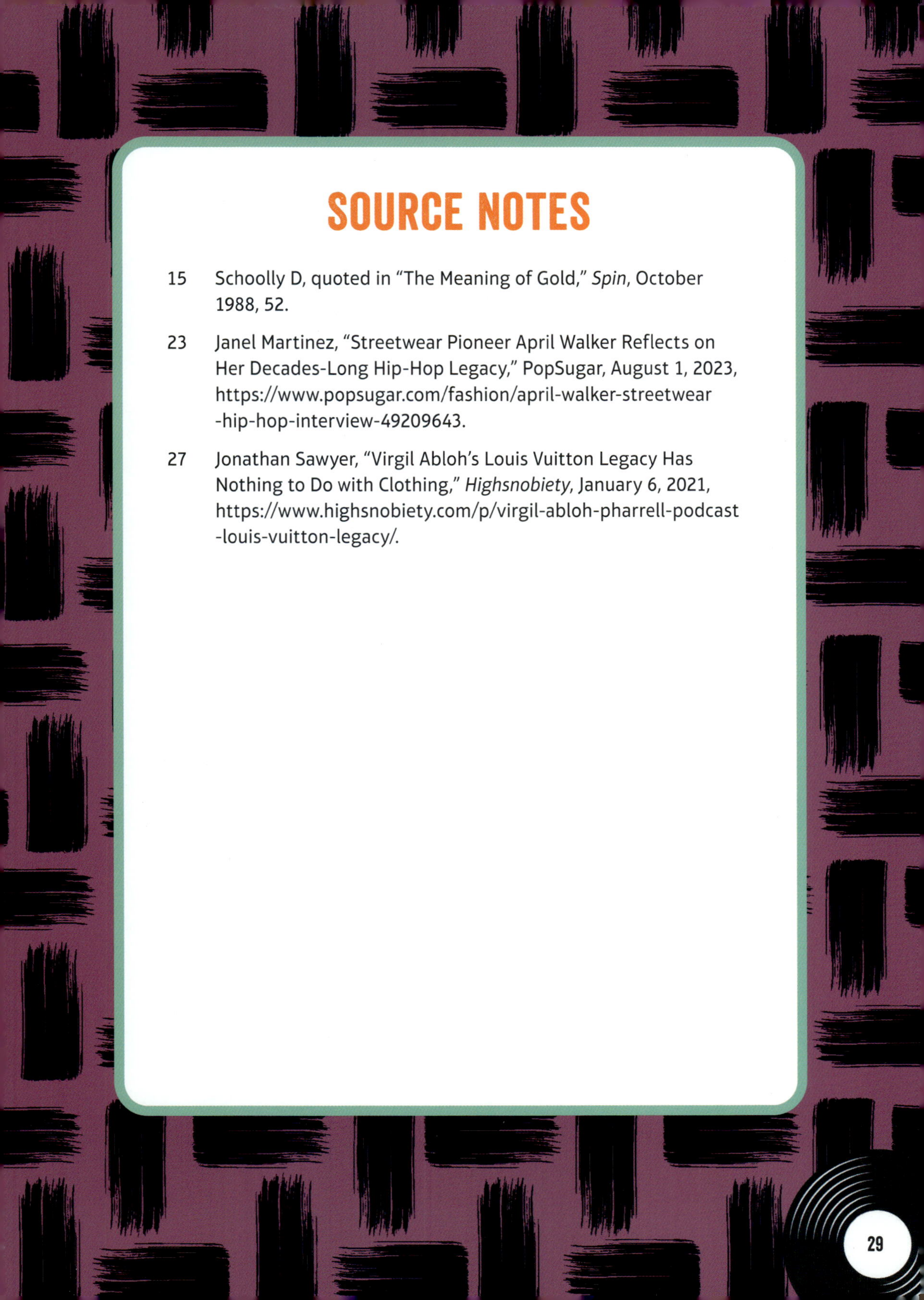

SOURCE NOTES

15 Schoolly D, quoted in "The Meaning of Gold," *Spin*, October 1988, 52.

23 Janel Martinez, "Streetwear Pioneer April Walker Reflects on Her Decades-Long Hip-Hop Legacy," PopSugar, August 1, 2023, https://www.popsugar.com/fashion/april-walker-streetwear-hip-hop-interview-49209643.

27 Jonathan Sawyer, "Virgil Abloh's Louis Vuitton Legacy Has Nothing to Do with Clothing," *Highsnobiety*, January 6, 2021, https://www.highsnobiety.com/p/virgil-abloh-pharrell-podcast-louis-vuitton-legacy/.

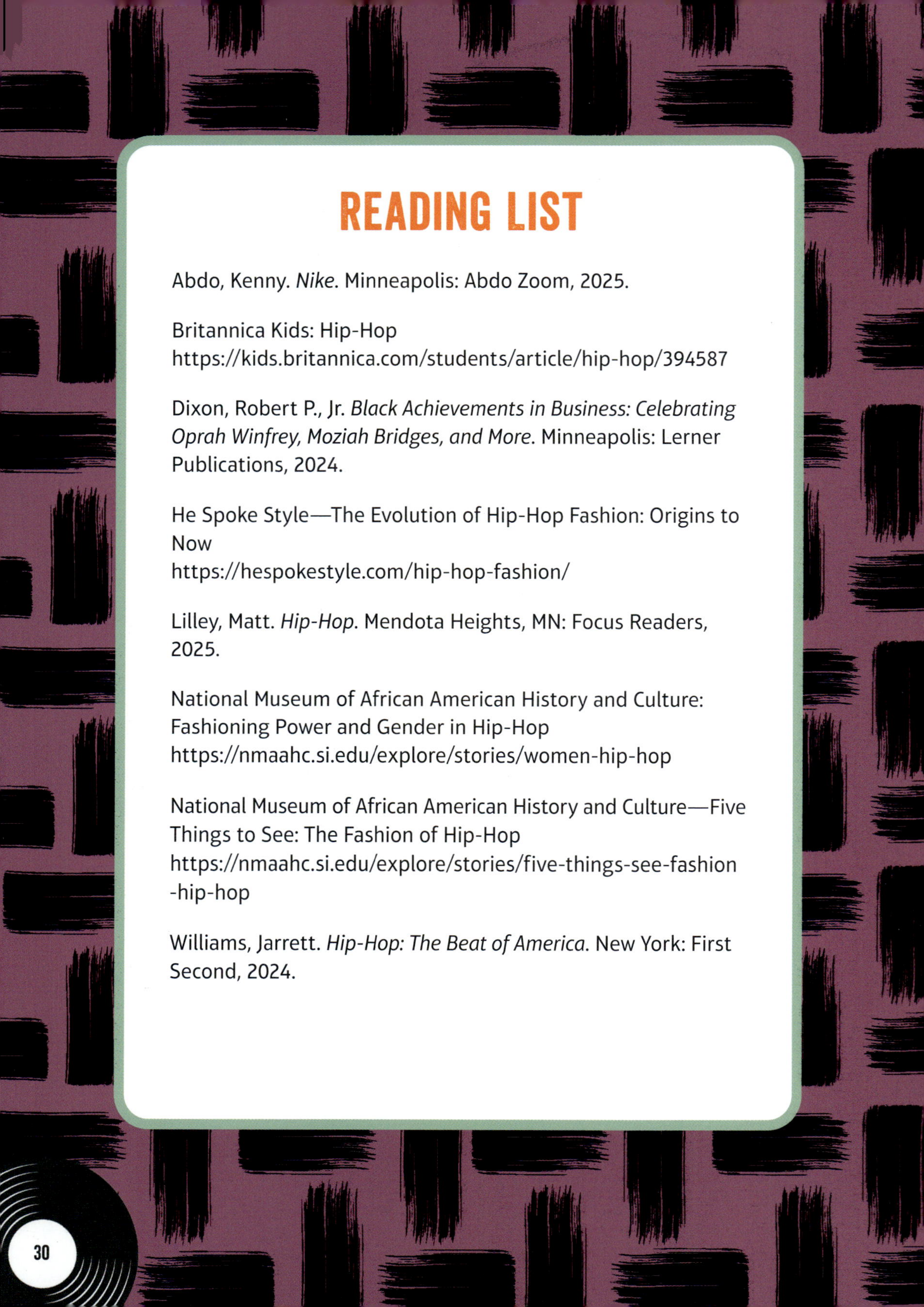

READING LIST

Abdo, Kenny. *Nike*. Minneapolis: Abdo Zoom, 2025.

Britannica Kids: Hip-Hop
https://kids.britannica.com/students/article/hip-hop/394587

Dixon, Robert P., Jr. *Black Achievements in Business: Celebrating Oprah Winfrey, Moziah Bridges, and More*. Minneapolis: Lerner Publications, 2024.

He Spoke Style—The Evolution of Hip-Hop Fashion: Origins to Now
https://hespokestyle.com/hip-hop-fashion/

Lilley, Matt. *Hip-Hop*. Mendota Heights, MN: Focus Readers, 2025.

National Museum of African American History and Culture: Fashioning Power and Gender in Hip-Hop
https://nmaahc.si.edu/explore/stories/women-hip-hop

National Museum of African American History and Culture—Five Things to See: The Fashion of Hip-Hop
https://nmaahc.si.edu/explore/stories/five-things-see-fashion-hip-hop

Williams, Jarrett. *Hip-Hop: The Beat of America*. New York: First Second, 2024.

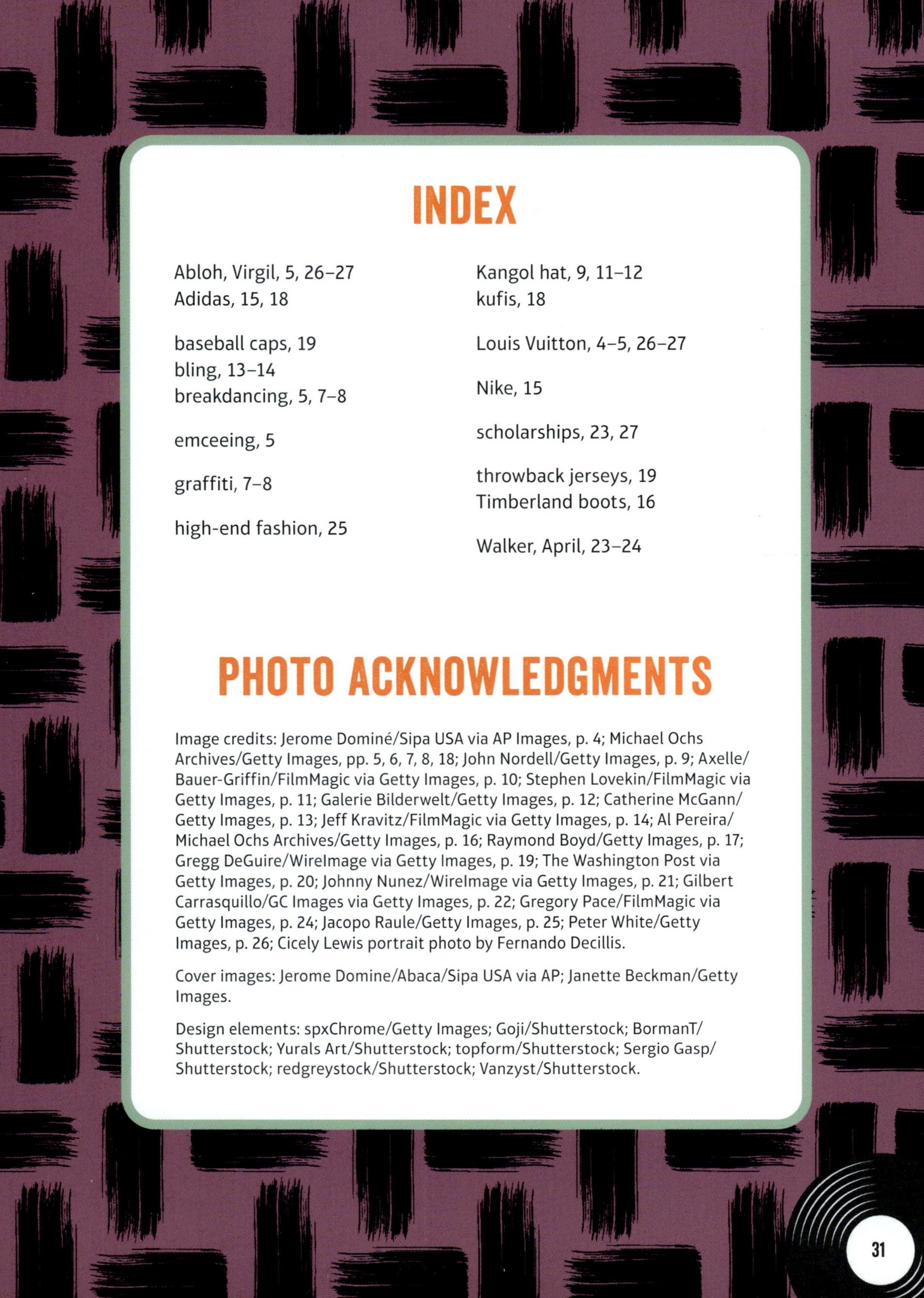

INDEX

PHOTO ACKNOWLEDGMENTS

Image credits: Jerome Dominé/Sipa USA via AP Images, p. 4; Michael Ochs Archives/Getty Images, pp. 5, 6, 7, 8, 18; John Nordell/Getty Images, p. 9; Axelle/Bauer-Griffin/FilmMagic via Getty Images, p. 10; Stephen Lovekin/FilmMagic via Getty Images, p. 11; Galerie Bilderwelt/Getty Images, p. 12; Catherine McGann/Getty Images, p. 13; Jeff Kravitz/FilmMagic via Getty Images, p. 14; Al Pereira/Michael Ochs Archives/Getty Images, p. 16; Raymond Boyd/Getty Images, p. 17; Gregg DeGuire/WireImage via Getty Images, p. 19; The Washington Post via Getty Images, p. 20; Johnny Nunez/WireImage via Getty Images, p. 21; Gilbert Carrasquillo/GC Images via Getty Images, p. 22; Gregory Pace/FilmMagic via Getty Images, p. 24; Jacopo Raule/Getty Images, p. 25; Peter White/Getty Images, p. 26; Cicely Lewis portrait photo by Fernando Decillis.

Cover images: Jerome Domine/Abaca/Sipa USA via AP; Janette Beckman/Getty Images.

Design elements: spxChrome/Getty Images; Goji/Shutterstock; BormanT/Shutterstock; Yurals Art/Shutterstock; topform/Shutterstock; Sergio Gasp/Shutterstock; redgreystock/Shutterstock; Vanzyst/Shutterstock.

Copyright © 2026 by Lerner Publishing Group, Inc.

All rights reserved. International copyright secured. No part of this book may be reproduced, stored in a retrieval system, or transmitted in any form or by any means—electronic, mechanical, photocopying, recording, or otherwise—without the prior written permission of Lerner Publishing Group, Inc., except for the inclusion of brief quotations in an acknowledged review.

Lerner Publications Company
An imprint of Lerner Publishing Group, Inc.
241 First Avenue North
Minneapolis, MN 55401 USA

For reading levels and more information, look up this title at www.lernerbooks.com.

Main body text set in Aptifer Sans LT Pro.
Typeface provided by Linotype AG.

Editor: Annie Zheng

Library of Congress Cataloging-in-Publication Data

Names: Morall-Baker, Monica B., author.
Title: Hip-hop style : fashion forward / Dr. Monica B. Morall-Baker.
Description: Minneapolis : Lerner Publications, [2026] | Series: Hip-hop culture | Includes bibliographical references and index. | Audience: Ages 9–14 | Audience: Grades 4–6 | Summary: "Hip-hop fashion has its roots in New York City, but since its birth it's become part of global mainstream culture. From accessories to hip-hop artist collabs, learn more about hip-hop fashion's trends and history"—Provided by publisher.
Identifiers: LCCN 2024037296 (print) | LCCN 2024037297 (ebook) | ISBN 9798765659847 (library binding) | ISBN 9798765684276 (paperback) | ISBN 9798765678015 (epub)
Subjects: LCSH: Fashion design—Juvenile literature. | Hip-hop—Influence—Juvenile literature.
Classification: LCC TT507 .M6555 2026 (print) | LCC TT507 (ebook) | DDC 746.9/2—dc23/eng/20250113

LC record available at https://lccn.loc.gov/2024037296
LC ebook record available at https://lccn.loc.gov/2024037297

Manufactured in the United States of America
1-1011685-53631-2/4/2025